Doug Lugg, Boy Slug

Written by
Peter Bently

Illustrated by
Bill Ledger

OXFORD
UNIVERSITY PRESS

OXFORD
UNIVERSITY PRESS

Great Clarendon Street, Oxford, OX2 6DP, United Kingdom

Oxford University Press is a department of the University of Oxford. It furthers the University's objective of excellence in research, scholarship, and education by publishing worldwide. Oxford is a registered trade mark of Oxford University Press in the UK and in certain other countries

Text © Peter Bently 2015
Illustrations © Oxford University Press 2015

The moral rights of the author have been asserted

First published 2015

British Library Cataloguing in Publication Data
Data available

ISBN: 978-0-19-835643-1

10 9 8 7 6 5 4

Paper used in the production of this book is a natural, recyclable product made from wood grown in sustainable forests. The manufacturing process conforms to the environmental regulations of the country of origin.

Printed in China by Leo Paper Products Ltd

Acknowledgements

Series Advisor: Nikki Gamble
Illustrated by Bill Ledger
Designed by Kim Ferguson

Little Doug Lugg loved chips and baked beans.
He loved pizza and pies but he **hated** his greens.

Mum tried to tell Doug Lugg he was wrong.
"Eat all your greens and you'll grow **big** and **strong**.
You can't go and play till that plate is all finished.
I'm off to the garden to water my spinach."

There was only one thing that annoyed Mrs Lugg.
And that was the sight of a **slimy, fat** slug.
"I just can't believe it!" she said. "What a pain!
They're eating the plants in my garden again!"

5

A friendly old gardener was just passing by.
He said, "Here's a powder for slugs you can try.
It makes them feel funny. They hate it, I've found,
If you sprinkle a tiny bit over the ground.

SLUG-GONE

The best time to use it is six in the morning.
It'll sort out your problem. But one little warning:
It's **powerful** powder. Don't touch it yourself!
Please keep it safe on a very high shelf."

That night little Doug wanted something to drink.
So he crept to the kitchen and went to the sink.
But he tripped in the dark on the edge of a rug –
And the powder tipped over and fell onto Doug!

"What a very strange powder. It tickles!" Doug cried.

"And it's making me feel a bit *funny* inside!"

He felt himself changing and then he cried, "**Eeek!**"
As his skin started turning all slimy and sleek ...

SLUG-GONE

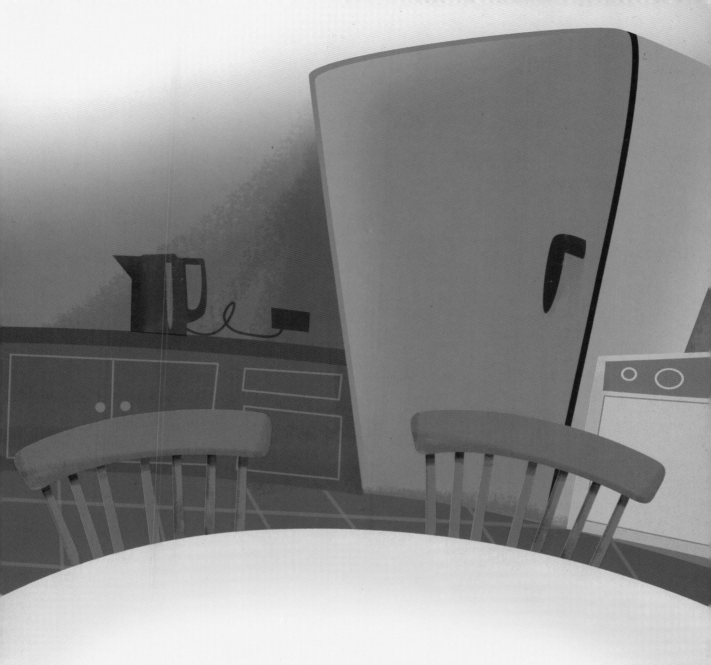

It took thirty seconds for little Doug Lugg
To change from a boy to a massive, great …

"I'm hungry!" said Doug, slipping over the floor,

And using his slug tail to open the door.

He slid down the path to the vegetable garden
And said to the slugs there, "I do beg your pardon,
It's been quite a while since I last had my tea
So is there a nice juicy cabbage for me?"

But as soon as the other slugs saw that great beast,
They turned round in terror and fled from their feast.
They slithered away just as fast as they could
To a nice slimy swamp far away in a wood.

15

Doug said, "I know! I'll find much more to eat
If I go to the shop at the end of the street."

He found the back door of the shop open wide.

"That's lucky," thought Doug as he slithered inside.

He slipped past the cookies, the cakes and the sweets,
The tarts and the ice creams and all kinds of treats.

Then he came to the vegetables, pile after pile,
And started to gobble them all with a smile.
Cabbages, **spinach** and **broccoli** too –
Nothing was left by the time he was through.

CHECKOUTS ▶▶

BROCCOLI

FRESH TODAY

SPINACH

CABBAGES

FRESH TODAY

19

But then Doug heard a sound. "I hear footsteps!" he cried.
"They're coming this way! I need somewhere to hide!"

The footsteps were made by a robber named Jack,
Who was just sneaking out with a sack on his back.

The robber had almost crept out of the store
When he saw a strange shadow quite close to the door.

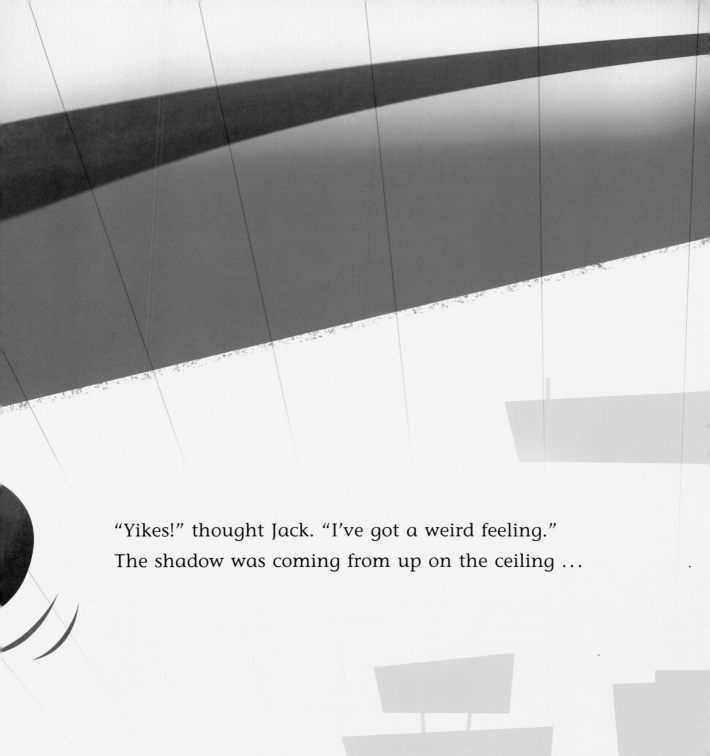

"Yikes!" thought Jack. "I've got a weird feeling."
The shadow was coming from up on the ceiling ...

"A monster!" yelled Jack and he started to dash
Back through the shop with his big sack of cash.

He smashed the front door and he hadn't run far
When he saw the police driving up in their car.
"Hey!" cried the officers, holding Jack tight,
"It's *you* who's been robbing the shops every night!"

SUPERMARKET

WANTED

POLICE

"Arrest me!" said Jack. "I don't really care,
As long as I'm safe from that creature in there!
A great monster slug thing! Look, there's its trail!
At least I'll be safe if you put me in jail!"

Well, they followed the slime-trail to see where it led . . .

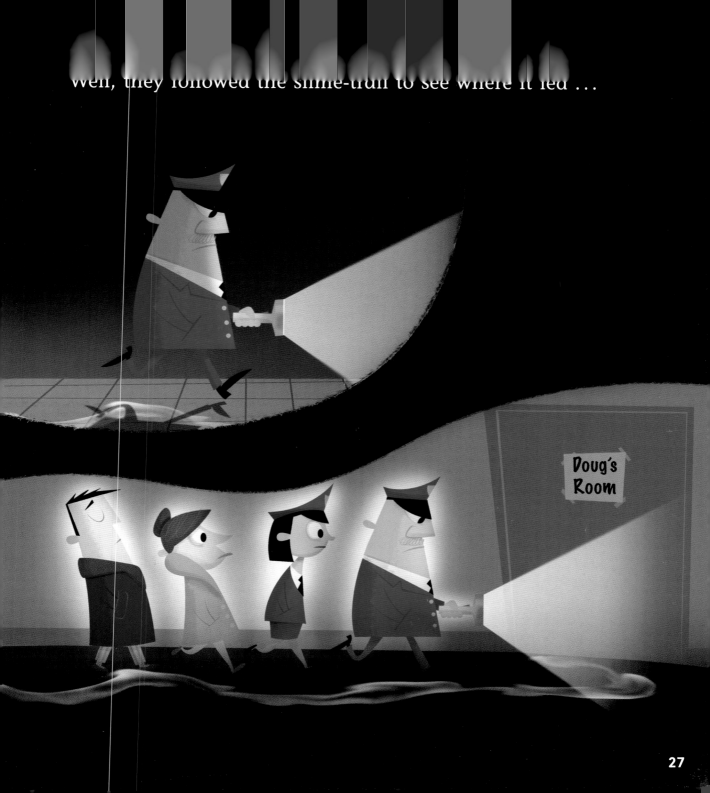

Doug's
Room

... But only found **Doug**, safely tucked up in bed.

"Look!" said the sergeant. "It's just little Doug.
Jack was pretending. There's no monster slug!"

The police were all pleased that the robbing had ended.
The next day, at lunch, Mrs Lugg said: "How splendid!
That powder has vanished – it's really quite weird –
But so have the slugs. They have all disappeared!"

But Doug Lugg just smiled as he happily ate
All the **broccoli**, **spinach** and **sprouts** on his plate.